13 MUST KNOW Principles for the Bar Exam

With any level of higher education, what you learn and how well you learn it for that particular field could become easier, if you understand the format in which it is instructed, and thus learned.

Hopefully you are reading this for the first time, and have never taken the bar exam before, either way preparation and details of the smallest type, are essential, just ask anyone who has been in your shoes before.

I wrote this publication in the hopes of providing a thought process for you to succeed. My other publications on this very subject, I share specifics that I have learned, that you must too, to give yourself the best opportunity to succeed, at the end of the day, that is really anyone can ask for.

In other publications, from this author, I will cover what I learned from a multitude of sources, and the reason why what used to be common protocol for exam takers, is now changing.

An example of what I mean is alleged to have occurred on the July 2014 bar exam. According to published sources, this class of examinees has the lowest pass rates in at least 10 years. What I have learned is that this low pass rate was arguably the fault of the National Committee of Bar Examiners (NCBE), and changes allegedly having been made to that particular exams MBE questions and answers. (For more information on this hot topic. *(Use the Google search engine, also find the response from at least one ABA Dean in a sharply worded letter to the NBCE on this matter.)*

One thing I learned is that if you are taking the next bar because you failed the first one, as was the case for me, learning and applying these 13 MUST KNOW items will make life for you a lot easier.

Before we get started, I wanted to take this

13 MUST KNOW Principles
for the Bar Exam

opportunity to thank all of my Colleagues from Harvard, and all of my law professors from around the country, Jay, George, Steve, Mary, Aaron, Jeff, and Alan, thanks for your help!!!

THE PRECEDING LOGO IS PART OF HARVARDS EFFORTS TO HAVE ALUMNI SHARE WHERE THEY ARE SHARING THEIR HARVARD EDUCATION, HERE I AM!!!

LEADERSHIP EXCELLENCE IMPACT

A. THOMAS ARCHIIR

13 MUST KNOW Principles
for the Bar Exam

1. Pay for the exam on the first date of eligibility, and reserve your hotel now. Most times you do not have to pay until you show up at the hotel. This is important because the closer you get to the day of the exam, the room rates go up tremendously, if you can find a room at all.

By taking care of these two items, it will allow you to focus on what you need to do and provide two less items to worry about. Also in many jurisdictions the date you pay for the exam, decides where you will sit.

Some law schools require that their students all pay for their bar exams on the same day, thus allowing for classmates to sit with one-another throughout the entire examination.

Those that wait until the last minute, will be sitting with all of the other procrastinators, in the back of the room, with the entrance and exit noise a constant distraction.

Besides, if you are a procrastinator at heart,

now is the time to stop that habit. Being a procrastinator in law can be quite expensive, especially when dealing with filing deadlines, and response due dates.

If this is you, break the habit now, get with your friends and pay together, study together when applicable, and clear this portion of the preparation from your to do list, then study with confidence. This is probably the only thing close to any control you may have for the exam.

2. Understand where your education to take the bar comes from. This is important because of the history of the exam, and pass rates.

Researching the history of the exam as it applies to those on the edge of legal education, meaning a non-ABA education, or those who struggle through the ABA schools.

This is essential, and if history repeats itself, could be the difference between celebrating, or preparing again. So, know your type of schools' passing rates, the Bar does, and they use history such as this in ways beyond imagination. You should know what the bar knows about your type of school, and avoid pitfalls of learning provided historically by your school type. (In California there are many school types for bar exam eligibility, the bars' website breaks down the performance of each type of school, as it relates to the overall pass rate of the bar.)

Do not let your type of school become a hindrance to you. Give yourself the best opportunity to compete and pass by learning what the bar knows based on history.

For example, one of my college mates took the July, 2014 examination, and despite scoring an 86 in the MBE portion of the exam, the bar failed him and scored him at 1420, when 1440 is needed.

Some Bar organizations allow for examinees to have a review by the committee if their overall score is within a certain percentage of passing, so learn what category your school is in, and be prepared.

For this reason, knowing how your school is classified by the bar may provide a much needed platform of issues to raise, as to why your score should be adjusted in your favor.

Below is an example of a breakdown that

shows how the bar knows who you are, by the type of school you have attended:

"As expected, the applicants who had the most success on the July test were those who had attended California law schools approved by the American Bar Association. Sixty-nine percent of first-time test-takers and 23 percent of repeat test-takers from ABA-accredited schools in California passed the test. Those numbers for out-of-state ABA-accredited schools were 60 percent and 14 percent, respectively.

More detailed statistics showing how test-takers at individual law schools fared are expected to be released in January and will be available on the State Bar website. *(Source: California Bar)*

NOTES:

13 MUST KNOW Principles for the Bar Exam

3. Know all sources of alternative bar preparation. This means that the test taker MUST be familiar with all styles of test taking. If you are a repeater, one style is not enough, so think about adding other sources of bar preparation like, Themis, BarMax, Adaptibar, Kaplan, CaliforniaBarHelp.com, Fleming, 1440calbarhelp, etc. There are many sources available to you, so check them out, try to find a fit, and learn from them, even if it is just one thing.

Adding more than one bar tutor while studying will place you in the best possible situation on exam day to pass, because you will be familiar with more than one method, and thought process. The bar exams can differ greatly, and learning how to approach each individual essay question, will provide you with more options on how to write for that question.

Also as important, is to make friends with

13 MUST KNOW Principles for the Bar Exam

others who are also taking the exam, they may have resources of materials you do not, and Vise-versa, this is a must do, no matter how difficult, this is a matter of life and your own personal growth.

At this point, I want to give-a-shout-out to my study partners, you can ad yours below. A special thank you to Don, John, Steve, Sophie, Stanley, and most importantly my wife, Cindy.

Ad Your Study-Partners Names and Contact information Below:

4. If you are using a computer on the bar exam, it is essential that you familiarize yourself with the software before the date of the exam. This is very important because the features of underline, bold, and italicize should be used in your presentation to the grader of your work.

By learning how to work the software, you can easily go back to a previous exam, maybe to cut-and-paste, or to make sure you remembered to write a key point of the previous exams. Learn how it works now, familiarize yourself with all available functions, such as spell check, and auto-correct.

While in the middle of my exam, I recalled that earlier when writing on a Murder, on a previous essay, I suddenly remembered that I had failed to define Homicide. This omission could have failed my entire exam, but I knew how to get back to that essay, because I had practiced, and beat up the software while in

13 MUST KNOW Principles
for the Bar Exam

the comfort of my own home. Thus I was able to go back to that earlier saved essay with confidence, and I added my definitions of Homicide, then moved, back the middle of my other essay.

Do not be afraid to call the manufacturer of the software and ask questions. I did, and the wait was not too long, and the representative seemed knowledgeable, patient, and willing to assist.

Important to note that when you are sitting in the exam, and the proctor tells the examinees to open the software, a new
screen will appear that is slightly different from the one you studied.

When this happened to me, it scared me beyond belief, because the screen prompt was requesting a password to enter the exam software. All of the passwords I tried failed, and because the "no talking warning: had been given by the proctor, I had no one to ask about this.

I started to really worry that I would have to hand write my exam, and my mind began to race, because I had not ever practiced handwriting any exam in law school before. Thankfully and eventually the proctor announced to the examinees where the password for this examination could be found. It was on one of the pages in our exam hand-outs. So, in the event this happens on your exam, do not be like me, as you now will know that you are not alone, and where to find your password.

5. Be open to learning more theories and applications of law, because on the exam, one theory or application may not fit perfectly, but another will. Here you will find differences in legal argument, and on the exam, if what you learned does not fit, another angle of the same area of law, may, but you must trust those other sources, so "learn it and confirm it," this can go a long way, especially under stress.

One of my additional or alternative law professors likes to use these foreign or weird names for the actors names in his essays. This used to drive me crazy, making me think "can't you just keep everything simple," after all you are naming the parties.

While reading with comprehension necessary to understand the essay, I now have to worry about how to pronounce this name, or think of another name to give that actor.

What I have since learned is that this is a very

effective way to teach what you will probably face on the bar exam, and studying before hand will allow you to understand and thus react to the style of the author, and what is expected to be a passing answer.

One professor told me, that since he is writing the essay, he knows the model answer, this is true for the bar graders too, so practice essays with the funny city, or weird actors names in them, and be better prepared for those weirdos, when you see them on the bar exam.

6. Get a copy of the testable material that will be given on each day of the exam. This means that Monday's exam consists of these applications, Tuesday of this and Wednesday of that. Then, while practicing, place yourself mentally in the exam at that time, keep an eye on your clock, then realize what you are missing, or what is lacking. It is better to find that out now, remember it, correct it, and apply it.

While discussing this area of preparation, I think it is important to tell you that memorandum writing is alive and well at the bar.

I hope by this time in your preparation, that you are familiar with how to write all areas that will be tested, and that you practice writing all that will be written. Come exam day, you will be familiar with all of the different styles and formats in which you will be tested.

13 MUST KNOW Principles for the Bar Exam

The "Memorandum," (performance tests) requires attorney style skills to complete, and is the most over-looked practice by law students, according to my many sources. For this reason, you may want to look at getting a tutor, who has a specialty in this type of writing, and you must not ignore it, if you do, you may find yourself learning it for the next exam, and note that your exam may vary by jurisdiction. *(Example below)*

"The three-day General Bar Examination is given twice a year, in February and July. The exam consists of three sections: a multiple-choice Multistate Bar Examination (MBE), six essay questions and two performance tests that are designed to assess an applicant's ability to apply general legal knowledge to practical tasks." *(source California Bar website)*

13 MUST KNOW Principles
for the Bar Exam

NOTES:

7. Use Google, and the plain text rule when looking to find the law, this does work, and for students who are not already familiar with "Secondary Sources," familiarize yourself with this essential area and source of learning. CALI lessons offers an interactive tutorial specifically on this major growth area of learning, and preparing for the bar exam.

This all goes to the heart of diversity, and preparation. Learning one major point of law from secondary sources, can tie up a lot of lose-ends in your understanding of the law, but be careful to not go overboard on it.

I can remember my professor telling a story about students she went to law school with. With excitement she stated how those students could tell you about all of the new laws at every level, and that many of them would discuss the ramification of the new law, and it's affect on the modern world. She went on to point out, that not one of those students, ever passed the bar, and none of them are attorneys today.

This is kind of a sad story on one hand, but on the other hand, they failed to learn how to apply that knowledge to passing the exam.

Know your itinerary for each day, when possible, study that way, meaning practice learning in the way you will be tested. If it is writing first, then multiple choice, then study that way, because familiarity-breeds-comfort, I personally believe that statement too.

8. Do not be an "undercover law student." This means that those you come in contact with, must understand what you are trying to achieve, you will get heartfelt words of encouragement, and stories about so-and-so who did finally pass. Most of all the people in your lives will understand, that what you are trying to achieve, is a Nobel act, reserved for the brightest minds in the world, yes that is you...

One of my colleagues from law school shared a story about how he ran across a tutor, and was given a bunch of study material, by someone who had just passed the bar.

He said that he had been looking to move closer to his job, and found a home that was perfect for him, In talking with the parties, he mentioned that he was in school, and would soon be taking the bar. A young lady present then exclaimed that she had just passed the bar, and had been recently sworn-in. She went on to say that it was her aunt who tutored her, and then offered the same that she studied with, to my classmate. This classmate passed the exam on the first try, and developed life long friendships with two other local attorneys.

Another thing I found helpful was to join your local bar, as a student member. The cost is around $30, and you get all of the benefits associated membership as an attorney. This includes, magazines, free webinars, and social events reserved just for bar members. I have met many great people this way, and I consider them to be friends, they also appear to be happy to discuss, and help me with the law, when I need understanding.

I also have added music when studying from secondary sources, or other non-complex legal matter. I created a music list that contains what I consider to be songs adhesive to my learning. I use Spotify, which is free and created my own mini radio station, my site contains music that is positive, motivational, and yet conducive to learning for me. So if you feel the need, take the time, and create your own music to study by, it helps time pass, and before you know it, you will have covered a multitude of legal theories and applications. Hopefully some of what you learned may be the difference between a pass, or a retake for your bar exam.

NOTES:

9. Understand that in law, "Gut-Feelings" are not enough for the exam, while it is okay to use them now, at testing time they should be a very last resort on exam day.

Generally gut-feelings can be a great way to win at a Black Jack table, or on the roulette wheel, many times they may pay off for you.

Please note that on your bar exam, the professors who write the exams, generally write them to allow you the comfort of going with your gut-feelings, and most of the time when you do that, you will be wrong.

The authors of the exam, have months, and years to write these exam questions, and you only have an hour to answer them, so be prepared to overcome this temptation, or lazy way out.

Understanding the difference between the words, shall, must, could, may, as they apply to legal writing, and understanding of the law is essential. So make sure you do know these differences when you read them in your essay, it could be the difference between a correct writing, and one not so correct.

One of my favorite Professor's once told me the following quote;

"When you have eliminated the impossible, no matter how improbable, what is left must be the truth." This is especially important when process of elimination is what you are faced with, and is better than any gut-feeling, so please make a post card, place that quote in your memory, and apply it, instead of your gut-feelings.

10. When in doubt look for the law, logic, and facts, for an appropriate response. Understand the power of "legal fiction," and when, how, where, or if, you should apply this powerful knowledge.

The term "legal fiction," is generally defined as: An assumption that something has occurred or someone or something exists which, in fact, is not the case, but that is made in the law to enable a court to equitably resolve the matter before it. In order to do justice, the law will permit or create legal fiction. *Legal Dictionary by Farlex 2014*

One recent use of legal fiction appears in a recent law suit filed against the state bar of California.

On the cover of the pleading, listed under the words Defendant's appears the word ROES 1-50. My first thought was this was a typo, but then I remembered the attorney is a prominent attorney with national recognition,

A. THOMAS ARCHIIR

and the defendant is the State Bar of California.

Most of us are readily familiar with the term DOES as it applies to legal pleadings, but ROES...

For some of you this may be a poor example of legal fiction, but on the exam when posed with essays that include, Urbania, or other fictional statements as facts, researching words such as ROE, could have provided for you a vein of other similar legal fiction words.

Unfortunately, and unmistakably, this is the reality in which we are being tested today, and learning this area of law, may be the only thing you can use in a pinch, that at least has a resemblance of legal authority.

NOTES:

11. You MUST make time to STUDY, this means physically every hour available. The easiest way to do this is to study in a method or approach that will allow you to learn.

Some people are readers only, and do not, or, cannot listen to the lectures or definitions via audio publications, but instead must read them to understand, or are more comfortable just reading, or Vice-versa. Just like reading is important, audio is just as important, because the same way you learn to sing the words to your favorite song, can be applied to learning and recalling the law.

For others who audio provides their best learning environment, you must read, and learn how exam passers are formatting the passing essays, see every period, comma, and high-lighted areas. Remember, Success, breads success, and you must help yourself, at every opportunity, and learn what you must learn to pass, no exceptions!!!

With respect to the difficulties in understanding the law and issues which occurs sometimes, one of my favorite professors states; "you have no choice but to understand it."

So make sure when preparing that you find a way to understand what you are reading, because on the exam, you will be faced with far-fetched facts, with many actors, and laws, but by practicing the difficult readings now, you will have the mind set and confidence to remain competitive during the exam.

12. When practicing and taking the exam, do not leave the law or legal rules in your head, put it on paper. The following words should never be part of your legal academia, "I knew that." Do not assume the grader knows what you know. You must show them that you not only know that law or rule, but also how it applies to the facts in the essay.

On a recent exam, the facts had children who were intentionally and negligently injured, by a plaintiff.

On the call of the question, you were asked what legal rights and remedies the children had, they were 6, 7, and 8 years old.

After the exam was published, it hit the class rooms for discussion. The professor had been provided both failing exams, and passing ones from students who had sat for that exam, he advised that the students had been given scores by the bar ranging from 55 to

80.

Many of the essays were about the same length in pages, but the passing answers, had more law, law that all of us know, but those that did not pass, apparently did not feel at the time of the examination those laws were appropriate, or important enough to write about.

One difference between the 60 answer and the essays scored above 70 was two well known and simple areas of law, that would have taken minutes to cover. They were guardian ad litem, and substantial factor test, also *the passing answers had smaller paragraphs, but essentially the same content...*

13. Do not write on any essay more than one-hour. If you must then write no more than a maximum of an additional 3 minutes. The essays, by design will bring about thought that you could write on for several hours, and maybe even all-day. But those who have been successful on the examination, strictly adhere to the one-hour time allotment.

The more comfortable you are at the exam, the better and more focused you will be during times of stress.

For this reason, find the watch you are going to use on exam day. Remember in most jurisdictions the watch must be analog, as the other types are generally forbidden, and use it now as your time-piece to practice with, and again, stick-to-the-one-hour-time-limit, no matter how difficult.

On my recent exam, I had only 9 minutes to

go in order for me to adhere to the one hour mandate.

My third call of the question was "discuss defenses for the schizophrenic defendant."

This means that I had 9 minutes to write in IRAC format all four insanity defenses.

This provided, by design, a perfect chance for me to go over the time limit, but I knew if I did, history has shown I will not have enough time for the last essay of the exam.

I wrote all of the four insanity defenses in about 13 minutes, while well aware of my remaining time, but I also knew the last essay was going to be a full work-out requiring ever bit of an hour to complete.

Near the end of the last exam for the day, the proctor gave the examinees the "5 minute warning," over the loud speaker.

With just 5 minutes left on my last exam, I

still had to write an entire remedies section, for a breach of contract essay.

Just as I highlighted the rubric, "Remedies for Breach of Contract for Plaintiff," time was called, meaning if you touch your keyboard, you will be written up for cheating, which is not a good way to get your law career started.

For this reason you must learn to strictly-adhere to the one-hour-time frame now, because at the exam, learning about how much you can write in an hour, may be too late...

It should also be noted, that the **software for the exam has a built in clock timer,** you can use it also as I did. When I began to *outline* the essay, prior to writing the essay, I set the *timer for 15 minutes.*

When the software timer goes off, the screen of the computer will turn red on the right of the typing surface. You can set this time by minutes, or seconds, and I used it twice to add my 3 additional minutes, but made up for that time, in the "outline" portion of exam writing. How you use this timer is up-to-you, but it is a tool that is available, and you should practice using it before the exam takes place.

If you are going to pass, you must also do the same, because if you fail to comply with the one-hour per essay rules of the exam, it more-than-likely will result an academic disaster for the foreseeable future. Remember, "time-is-of-the-essence," as a little legal fiction designed to remind you of the one-hour academic mandate for successful bar essay writing.

Time is a serious issue, and failure to comply will assure that you will not complete an essay, thus an incomplete examination. If you allow this to happen, and do not complete all exams, this will almost always guarantee a failed result on the writing, leaving the far-fetched but achievable means of passing the exam, based on a strong performance on other portions of the test.

To learn more about MUST KNOW pointers for writing for the bar exam, please visit Amazon, or Kindle Books, look for more publications by A. Thomas Archiir and increase your knowledge, thus chances of being more effective, and better prepared on exam week.

You can make a difference in your quality of life and overall retention, by adding these concepts **to your daily study "regimen."**

My publication called "Take the confusion out of writing for the Baby Bar," is also a good source for any examinee, and covers the IRAC method of legal writing.

My publication on secondary sources, and using legal fiction to your advantage on the bar exam, will provide you with many valuable resources to place you in the best possible light for success. *(Please check for availability.)*

This publication is for educational purposes only, and represents my experience, but remember this is your exam, and you must prepare using many sources of information, due to the ever-changing examination formats, and both the required and expected contents, that you exam answer must contain.

Because of this I recommend using the many alternate methods of learning academic law as a good solid foundation, and remember this, learn-it-then-confirm-it, the law that is...

Please realize that the results of your exam, is in your hands, and preparation, repetitiveness, and legal logic MUST become a substantial factor if you are planning on passing your Bar Examination.

GOOD LUCK!!!

NOTES:

www.ingramcontent.com/pod-product-compliance
Lightning Source LLC
Chambersburg PA
CBHW070720180526
45167CB00004B/1558